SHAPING THE SOUL:

An Artist Collective

Jennie Denney

&

16 Gifted Artists

DEDICATION

Thank you to my family whose support and encouragement in this writing process keeps me going.

Thank you to the artists who contributed to this project, who encouraged me and brought depth, color, and meaning to each practice, and whose artistic input and prayers throughout this process were vital in bringing this journal together.

Thank you, Lord. For without You I would be one lost soul. Your goodness, grace, and love for me have changed my heart, soul, and mind. I'm so grateful.

My Dear Friend,

Spiritual practices are purposeful actions we can incorporate into our daily, weekly, monthly, and annual rhythms that create room for the Holy Spirit to transform our inner lives. While the Holy Spirit does the work, I firmly believe we have a part to play, and that is being present and purposeful in our time with the practices we choose to spend time on. They are the conditioning and the workout of our spirituality, where the Holy Spirit slowly and gently transforms us into Christlikeness.

Last year, I began searching for various ways I could connect with God. In this search, I found myself drawn to spiritual practices where I could experience Him through my five senses. It was through the purposeful actions of watching, searching, looking, feeling, touching, smelling, breathing, listening, hearing, tasting, and savoring, that I found grounding to my inner self in the present moment. In this search for spiritual practices, I wanted to be purposeful to make sure each way could become a practice I would be able to incorporate into my day-to-day, weekly, monthly, and annual rhythm.

As I began to incorporate practices into my own life and share the practices with others, I learned how many people were craving new and old ways to meet with God. I learned how we all need to be reminded that God is here with us. I learned how much we all need to be assured of God's love for us and how much joy we bring Him. I also learned that most of us struggle with being present.

Over time, I began to think of ways these practices could be put together into a journal. Because beauty has a tendency to draw me to wonder, I wanted to be sure this journal would have a strong and colorful artistic element to it. I put a call out to artists to see if anyone would be willing to bring the practices to life through their art. My hope was to have artists take one of the practices I had put together, practice it, pray over it, and be inspired to create a piece of artwork that reflected what that practice meant to them. This call resulted in 16 artists coming together to take my vision and create this unique journal that you now have in your hands.

My goal for this journal is four-fold:

1. The practices are meant to create space for the Holy Spirit to work in your life, molding and shaping you, so you can become more like Him.
2. The artwork is meant to create a Visio Divina experience. I believe images are powerful and have a way of teaching us to be present and more aware of what God is doing. I pray each artistic reflection brings life to the practice for you.
3. The lined paper is to give you space for writing, prayer, and reflection. After all, what is a journal without space for writing?
4. The blank page is for doodling. Some find doodling to be a way to express their inward feelings best. I wanted to be sure to include a blank page for each practice for those of you who find doodling to be a meaningful spiritual practice.

I pray this journal is a blessing to you. I pray that it reminds you of God's boundless love for you, provides the space you need to experience God's grace and goodness, and teaches you new ways you can be present and available to the ways God is moving deep within your soul.

With love,

Your Sister in Christ and Fellow Traveler,

Jennie Denney

Table of Contents

Find a leaf whose color has turned.
Notice the color.
Notice the shape.
Notice the lines, stem, and tips.
How does the leaf feel?
Can you tell what tree it came from?

by: Kim Litchi

Allow that leaf to be a reminder of how much God
delights in every detail of your outer and inner life.

What is something that brings you great joy?

Make a list of things that bring you joy.

Take one of the things on your list and do it.

by: Brook Blanton

It makes God smile when we do things that bring us

deep joy!

We could all use a blessing every once and a while.

"MAY the *Lord* BLESS *you* & KEEP *&you;* the *Lord* MAKE *his face* Shine UPON YOU & BE *gracious* TO YOU; the *Lord* TURN HIS *face* TOWARD YOU & give *you peace.*"

— NUMBERS 6:24-26 —

CASEY HILTY | 2021

by: Casey Hilty

Find someone, look them in the eye, and bless them.

Find something you find to be beautiful.

by: Reagan Denney

Let it remind you of how much God delights in you.

Your presence matters to others, and especially to God.

by: Carrie Watts

What are some ways God has been present to you?
What is something you can do to be completely present
for someone today?
What is one way you can be present to God?

Find a tree and walk around it.
Feel the bark.
What does it feel like? Can you describe its color?
Notice the curve of each branch.
Where is each one pointing to? Can you hear birds chirping
in the tree or a breeze rustling the leaves? Take a deep
breath. Is there a smell eminating from that tree?

by: DJ Hejtmanek

Pausing to notice something in nature that God has made can
be a good reminder of how much more he takes care of our
every need.

TRY TO MAKE SOMEONE ELSE

LAUGH

BY PRETENDING TO BE A

SILLY ANIMAL

by: Rachel Schelb

Close your eyes and take three slow, deep breaths.

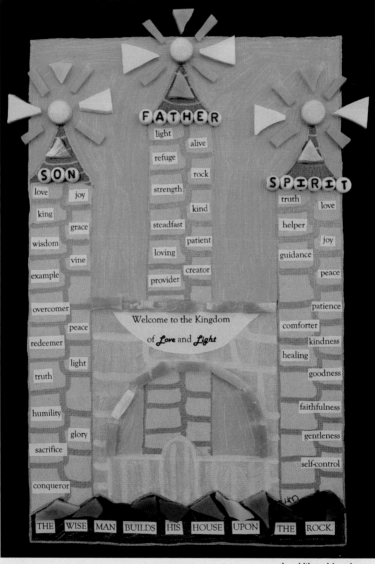

by: Hilary Mungle

Sometimes we need to be reminded of God's incredible character!

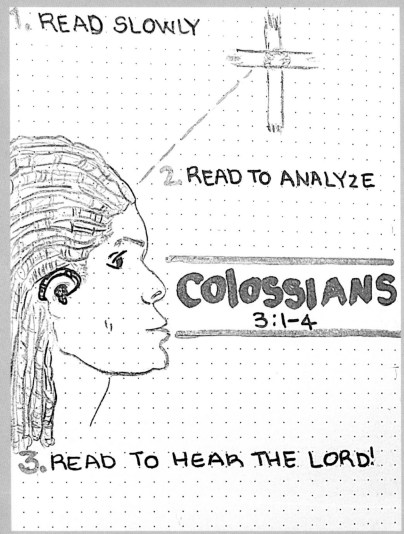

by: Sereta Collington

Read Colossians 3:1-4 again, paying attention to any
word or phrase that jumps out at you.
Read it one more time and ask the Lord what He would
like to say to you today through that word or phrase.

"...my cup overflows."

Psalm 23:5

by: Kim Blain

Write this verse out and take some time to memorize it throughout your day.

Songs can be powerful.

by: Kat Silverglate

Ask the Lord to place a song in your heart.

Take a moment to look at yourself in a mirror.
What do you see?
What do you notice?

by; Brenna Harter

Without losing eye contact, tell yourself,
"I am deeply loved by the God of the universe. He
delights in me. I am perfectly safe because He's got
me."

Read Psalm 59:9&10 three times slowly, pausing for a minute to contemplate the words each time.

by: Cassie Hubert

What do you think God might be saying to you through this verse?

by: Sara Sifre

Think of three moments in your day and reflect upon them.

High: When did you feel closest to God?

Low: When did you feel furthest from God?

Buffalo: What was something random or funny that happened?

Close your eyes, take a few deep breaths, and say
the following prayer:

by: Brianna Heida

"Lord Jesus Christ, Son of God, reveal yourself to me in
this moment."
Open your eyes and wait in expectation for Him.

Take a walk today and make a list of how many things you can see, hear, feel, and smell around you.

by: Christina Zambrano

Sometimes we need to slow down and stand in awe at God's exquisite artistry.

"Keep me as the apple

of Your eye..."

Psalm 17:8

by: Kim Blain

Is there a word or phrase that resonates with you today?
Ask the Lord what He would like to say to you.

What is a simple thing you enjoy doing?
Is it dancing in the rain, reading your favorite book, eating
something sweet, or smelling a flower?

by: Brenna Harter

Take some time today to go do what it is that brings
you joy, and as you do it, remember the joy you bring to
our loving Father.

What has been the most difficult thing you have experienced lately?
What has been the greatest blessing?

by: DJ Hejtmanek

Sometimes we need to take a moment to name the hard and pair it with a blessing, remembering that God is with us.

NEXT TIME YOU TAKE A SIP OF COFFEE:

THINK ABOUT THE PROCESS IT TOOK FROM THE PLANTING OF THE LITTLE COFFEE BEAN TO WHAT YOU ARE HOLDING IN YOUR HAND.

SOMETIMES WE NEED TO SIT BACK AND STAND IN AWE AND WONDER AT THE PROCESS.

by: Rachel Schelb

Find a place where you can observe other people.

by: Christina Zambrano

What emotions are they displaying? How are
they interacting with those around them?
Take a moment to pray for them.

Artist Contributors

Kim Lichti lives on 5 acres in Central California with her husband of 37 years, a golden retriever and a rescue cat! She has 5 grown children, 1 granddaughter and another on the way! She is a watercolor artist and devotional writer who can be found on Instagram @kimlichti.

Brook Blanton is an artist, author, and educator that delights in making space at the table to honor everyone's story. She believes that burned dreams and wilderness seasons can not extinguish the deep love of our Creator. Through real-life ordinary experiences, she longs to invite others to know the depth of their worth and the beauty of their belonging. You can find her on Instagram @brookblanton and blogging at www.brookblanton.com

Casey Hilty is a Christian speaker, artist, worshipper, and author of Her Children Arise—A Bible Study for Moms. Using both storytelling and visual art, she is passionate about taking mothers on a journey from apathy to awe to fall in love—or back in love—with God and His Word. Her artwork serves as a vital part of her writing and speaking ministry by encouraging moms to adorn the walls of their homes with scripture and to utilize their own creative gifts to bring glory to God. Casey is a content partner for YouVersion, and a member of both hope*writers and L'Acadian Art Guild. You can connect with her on Instagram @caseyhilty, Facebook @caseyhilty1, and at www.caseyhilty.com.

Carrie Watts is a Wife, Mom, and works part time maintaining Commercial Real Estate. She enjoys early morning Sunrises, Coffee, and Quiet time. She was a practicing registered nurse until her children were born. In her quest to find community among other moms like her, she found Classical Communications Home School group while living in Alexandria, VA. When she moved home to Mississippi in 2010, she started Classical Communications in her area. She especially enjoyed learning the Essentials of Writing with her sons. While teaching her sons, she also improved her love for writing and art. The education for her sons blossomed into a new hobby for herself. She has been writing and shooting photos ever since. You can find her at www.StayHigh.blog.

Reagan Denney is an eighth grader who loves cows, art, and her dog Rusty. She enjoys drawing, reading, painting, playing Minecraft with her brothers and sister, and she is a budding YA author. When she grows up, she wants to rescue animals and help people. You can find her on Pintrest at @Lemonnssss.

DJ Hejtmanek is passionate about equipping people to walk in freedom, discover who they are and fulfill their calling in Christ. She is a development professional, currently raising funds for an international Christian organization. DJ has worn many hats – magazine editor, wife, radio broadcaster, blogger, Mom, public relations spokesperson, community college administrator, children's book author, Bible teacher, JoJo's dog trainer, "Dovie" to five little girls, and licensed minister. During the pandemic, DJ discovered a love for painting and is exploring this new creative medium and incorporating it into her ministry. Her website/blog can be found at www.djhejtmanek.com. She is on Instagram @djhejtmanek and Facebook @knowingyourgod. Transplants from Louisiana and Texas, DJ and husband Louis have been married 39 years, live in Broken Arrow, OK, and have two children and their families living nearby.

Rachel Schelb is incredibly passionate about the biblical call to show hospitality, or as she puts it – to love well on purpose. Through her blog and podcast, Rachel shares practical tips and biblical encouragement to do just that! She is an introvert who frequently gets confused for an extrovert. She loves tacos, breakfast food, Diet Dr. Pepper, and kayaking. Rachel has been married to her best friend, Andy, for 12 years, and they have two children. You can find her at www.rachelschelb.com, on Instagram @rachelschelb, and at her podcast: Love Well On Purpose available on all major podcast sites.

Hilary is a Christian artist, writer, Navy wife, and homeschooler. She grew up in southeast Missouri and the Navy has taken her family to Virginia, Florida, and now Japan. She loves deep conversations, chocolate, and polka dots. You can find her at www.awakemysoulart.com, on Etsy at www.awakemysoulawake.etsy.com, on Facebook at www.facebook.com/awakemysoulart and on Instagram at www.instagram.com/awakemysoulart.

Sereta Collington, better known as the journaling pastor, is a disciple of Christ who thrives as a wife, mother of three, pastor of Holy Trinity AME, puzzle lover, runner, Sherlock Holmes fan, teacher, and author of three inspiring books for those who seek to fall in love with the Bible: "Scripture Memorization Journal," "Becoming One with Christ" and "The Through Journal." Receiving a Master of Divinity from Knox Theological Seminary. Furthermore, she also has two Bachelor's degrees: A Bachelor of Arts in Humanities, a Bachelor of Science in Information Technology, and a Master of Education. Additionally, Rev Sereta is a presenter for many journaling workshops. To find out more, head on over to her website, www.seretacollington.com.

Kim Blain: The beautiful state of Montana has been her home for most of her life and she enjoys small-town living. She lives in a wonderful community and is thankful she and her husband were able to raise their three children there. Besides writing and speaking, she enjoys watercolor painting and using my creative talents to bless others through art. If asked, she would tell you her greatest blessings include her husband of over 30 years, her children and grandchildren, and walking with Jesus for 42 years.You can follow her art and writing at www.kimblain.com, on Facebook and Instagram at Kimberly J Blain and Plain Blain Design Co, and on Etsy at Plain Blain Design Co.

Kat Silverglate is a creative who brings the message of God's ridiculous love to the world through writing, speaking and the arts. Like a "Kat" with nine lives, she's an attorney, seminary grad, frequent speaker, writer, artist, wife, mother and founder of the nonprofit, The Ridiculous Hour Foundation, Inc., dedicated to inspiring lives ridiculously responsive to the promptings of God. You can find Kat at www.katsilverglate.com and www.theridiculoushour.com [launching in 2021].

Brenna Harter is mother to one son, Giovany. She lives in Wisconson. Brenna is an artist at heart and started her own business called Brenna Bonita Art in 2017. Most customers order paintings of their pets, but she takes any requests. Check her work out and she can be reached on Facebook at BrennaBonita.Art or on Instagram @brennabonita.art. You can also email her with questions at brennabonita.art@yahoo.com.

Cassie Hubert is a professional actor and singer who lives in the south of England, UK, with her husband and four children aged 9, 8, 6 and 1. She is currently based at home full-time, educating and raising her children. Additionally, Cassie is a poet, writer and coach -specialising in performance and communication skills, and she also offers coaching/mentoring for young mothers. You can find her words and thoughts over at createperformandmother.com on Instagram as Creativeperformermum and on Twitter and Facebook as create_mother.

With artistic people throughout both sides of her family, Sara Sifre had no choice but to be an artist herself. Creativity is simply in her blood. She finds joy in painting, collage, beading, shell hunting, and a good cup of coffee. Sara now lives in NC making soaps and lip balms while her two babies draw and sing beside her. You can find her at www.bonessoapco.com

Brianna Heida is a chronically-ill mama to four kiddos (two bio, two bonus) in the beautiful chaos of a blended family. She runs Painted Prayers, a nonprofit that teaches art as a spiritual practice. Ever the creative, she's built her life, her home, and her family with intention, love, and hand-crafted goodness. She can be found at her website at http://paintedprayers.org and on all the socials @briheida.

Christina Zambrano resides in NJ with her husband of 12 years and 11-year-old son. She writes encouraging fiction as well as real experiences she has encountered on her faith walk. At night, she transforms into a pediatric nurse. She can be found on Instagram @christina.zambrano_writes and at https://christinazambrano.com.